DECORATE
Your Denims

Contributing Writer: Susan Figliulo
Wearable Art Designers: Kristy Deutch, Hilary Elsinger

PUBLICATIONS
INTERNATIONAL, LTD.

Pictured on front cover, clockwise from top left: Cityscape *(see page 54)*, Charming Vest *(see page 21)*, Glitter Vest *(see page 12)* and Shredded 'n' Studded *(see page 14)*, and Sugar 'n' Spice *(see page 32)*.

Pictured on back cover: Dinosaur Dynasty *(see page 17)*.

Photography: Sam Griffith Studios

Band a Board™ is a trademark of Mark Enterprises. Berol® and Verithin® are registered trademarks of Berol USA, division of Berol Corporation. Crystal Gala Color™ is a trademark of Galacraft, Inc. Delta Fabric Dye,™ Delta Glitter™ Stuff for Fabric, Delta Shiny™ Opalescent Fabric Paint, and Delta Starlite Dye™ are trademarks of Delta/Shiva. Dusty Pilot® is a registered trademark of Dusty Pilot Creatives, Ltd., Inc. Fabric Painter™ is a trademark of Hunt Manufacturing Co. Floraguard™ is a trademark of Dusty Pilot® Creatives, Ltd., Inc. Galacraft Galafetti® is a registered trademark of Galacraft, Inc. Grumbacher Galaxy™ is a trademark of M. Grumbacher. Ivory Snow® is a registered trademark of Proctor & Gamble. Jazz-Ups™ is a trademark of Delight. Liquitex® is a registered trademark of Binney & Smith. Puttin' on the Glitz™ is a trademark of Mangelsen's. Scribbles® Dimensionals™ is a registered trademark and a trademark of Duncan. Speedball® is a registered trademark of Hunt Manufacturing Co. Tee-Board™ is a trademark of Acclaim. Tulip® and Fine Line Paint Writer® are registered trademarks of Tulip Productions. Tulip Candi Crystals,™ Tulip Fiber Fun!,™ Tulip Jumpin' Jeans,™ Tulip Liquid Glitter,™ and Tulip Slick Paint™ are trademarks of Tulip Productions. Westrim® is a registered trademark of Western Trimming Corp. Wonder-Under® and Pellon® are registered trademarks of Freudenberg Nonwovens, Pellon Division. X-Acto® is a registered trademark of Hunt Manufacturing Co.

The mention of products in directions is merely a record of the procedure used and is not intended as an endorsement.

Contents

Introduction

In the history of fashion, there's one word that will top the list of contributions from America—denim. From dungarees and dresses to caps and workers' overalls, denim is without question the all-American fabric.

Denim has been around for more than a century and shows no sign of losing its popularity. Indeed, denim is an absolute must in any wardrobe today.

Denim defines blue jeans; it's the fabric of choice for casual wear, the sturdy stuff of little boys' play clothes. It's what everyone wears for hanging around.

Denim is tough, adaptable, and just as attractive when washed nearly white as when brand-new. And denim has that wonderful, unique quality of adapting to its wearer's contours, making your clothes really yours.

There's another way to make your denims your own—decorate them. Crafting wearable art from denim clothes started with the patched and embroidered jeans made popular in the 1960s. Today, decorating denim is a statement of fun for just about anyone.

Many people think they could never master the tricks that produce incredibly attractive custom clothes. Decorating clothes seems too difficult, complicated, and technical. But this book will prove them wrong. We'll show how you can create great clothes easily and without great expense.

This how-to book was conceived and written for the beginner. We assume you don't know how to sew or how to paint. For each project, we tell you exactly what equipment we used—brand names included—to get the look we show. The key to our techniques is keeping it easy: gluing instead of sewing, painting instead of embroidering. With simple and detailed step-by-step photos, we explain every step thoroughly. And we give you ideas to adapt our work to your own tastes.

You'll like the fashionable variety we offer, from the Western look of a cowgirl's duster to a stunning cityscape encircling a jacket. Our vests alone are a super tour of the possibilities, from a funky glitter vest to a delicious confection in gold. We're especially proud of our children's clothes, which offer delightful ideas for little girls and little boys—not to mention their older sisters and brothers.

Most of all, we're proud to show the absolute beginner how to create these terrific looks. Anyone can follow our step-by-step directions and photographs. And we're certain you'll spend less time zipping through these designs than you'd spend shopping for a look you'd love as much. In the end, that's what it's all about: finding the look you love. It's much easier and more fun when you can do it yourself.

What You'll Learn

As you glance through the projects in *Decorate Your Denims*, you'll see some garments that are strictly for fun; you'll also see some pretty impressive clothes. But no garment is too complicated for the beginner. When we chose projects for this book, we followed one rule: Everything must be appropriate for the absolute beginner, the interested person with enthusiasm but little skill.

We stuck to techniques everyone is familiar with, such as gluing and simple painting. Don't be intimidated by the word "technique;" the word may mean nothing more complex than squirting paint from a tube and letting it dry. You needn't be scared off by projects that use more than one technique. In every project we explain exactly what to do. And photographs show how each step leads to a finished garment.

Following is a list of techniques used in our projects. This list will show the ideas behind the techniques and give you an idea of how these techniques work on denim. With a technique such as painting, for example, we don't explain every single use of painting as "basic painting" or "texture painting." Once you've read through the step-by-step directions, you'll see that the directions are quite clear without discussing technique.

We also list every bit of equipment you'll need for your project. Although we don't mention it, we hope you'll bring patience to every project. Our projects are easy, but they're not instant. If nothing else, most will require patience while the glue dries.

So, let's talk about the techniques you'll find in each project.

BASIC PAINTING: Using a brush or other tool to spread or otherwise manipulate paint or dye on a fabric surface. Generally, basic painting for our projects requires only one or two brushes. You'll see the few brushes we use and learn a little about each type of brush in our "What You'll Need" section below. In our list of equipment for each project, we identify the brand names of our paints and brushes. This lets you buy exactly what we used or find the most similar paint or brush by another maker. After you become more familiar with the brushes and equipment available for decorating denim, you may find that you come back to the same brushes over and over again.

TEXTURE PAINTING: Applying paint or dye to fabric to achieve a three-dimensional effect that is slightly raised from the fabric itself. Sometimes, texture painting is accomplished by simply placing paint from the tube directly onto the fabric and allowing the paint to dry where it fell. Most of the paints used in this book are dimensional paints; they are specially formulated to give a raised effect when placed right on fabric. We also like to use some specialized dimensional paints that contain an embellishing element such as glitter, small crystals, or tiny shreds of foil. These embellishing elements enhance the three-dimensional look when these paints dry.

PRINTING WITH PAINT: Applying paint or dye to fabric with a designed stamp. If you think back to the potato-stamping art projects you did as a child, you'll have the idea. This book contains just one printing with paint project—Dinosaur Dynasty. The project uses a sponge you can buy that is already cut in an amusing shape for a child's jacket. We coat the sponge with paint and use it as our stamp.

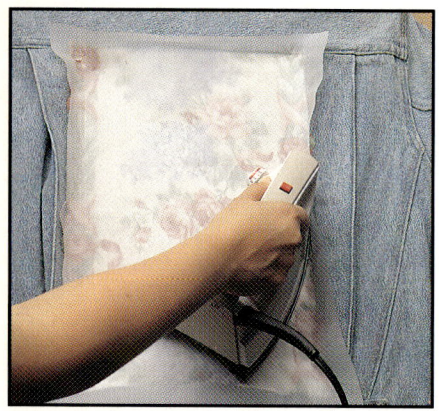

NO-SEW APPLIQUÉ: Affixing fabric to fabric using a medium, such as fabric glue, dimensional paint, or adhesive web, that causes them to adhere. Many products that adhere through application of heat are available in craft shops and variety stores.

When working with a garment, a shirt board will help keep the garment taut and in place (Charming Vest, page 21).

GLUING: Attaching fabric or embellishments to fabric using fabric glue or dimensional paint. Fabric glue is specially formulated to withstand washing. After the glue dries, it must be heat-set to keep its adhesiveness, and we tell you how to do this in each project. We also like to use dimensional paint, which has its own adherent properties, to attach or reinforce glued surfaces.

USING A SHIRT BOARD: Painting a fabric surface requires keeping that surface taut and flat. Although some denim garments are heavy enough to weight themselves, you must be sure the garment will stay put as you work. It's often best to use a shirt board, which is a wax-coated board you'll find discussed below in "What You'll Need."

When you use a shirt board, slide the board between the front and back of the garment you're about to paint. Be sure the waxy side of the board stays directly beneath the surface you plan to paint. If you're working on a shirt, jacket, or vest, button the front to maintain the line the finished garment will have and to help hold it in place. Then pull the arms of the garment snugly behind the board, being careful not to stretch the fabric so tightly that the garment's shape is changed. Use masking tape to fasten the arms onto the back of the jacket.

When working with a shirt, bring the bottom area up under the board and tape it to the back.

A vest or jacket may not need to be secured at the bottom. If it does, simply pull the bottom up as you did with the sleeves and tape the fabric in place. Although the back doesn't have to be neat, it should be as flat as possible so the garment lies evenly while you work on the front.

When painting a denim skirt, use a shirt board to hold the skirt taut by taping down one part of the skirt at a time. You'll usually want to decorate all around a skirt, so remember to let one painted area dry before taking the skirt off the board and taping the next area.

We sometimes suggest a design that covers more than the center location on a garment. To accomplish these variations, you may need a board that can accommodate a different shape. In the "What You'll Need" section, we explain how to make your own shirt board in the dimensions you need.

There you have it: six simple techniques that any beginner can master. Now you're ready to look at equipment.

What You'll Need

You won't need everything for every project. Some projects call for little more than a sharp pair of scissors and some fabric glue. But we want you to understand all the equipment mentioned in the projects. We've made a point of using only equipment that a beginner can obtain and master. Variety stores, craft shops, art supply stores, and even dime stores carry the equipment used here.

Since your store may carry only one line of the several paints and dyes we use in this book, we've given the type of paint or dye as well as the brand name. Brushes, too, come in different types by different manufacturers. In each project, we tell you the type of brush to use along with the manufacturer of the brush we used. We do the same for fabric glue, adhesive backing used for no-sew appliqué, and other products.

When your project requires paint or fabric dye, you'll need a palette, a cup of water to rinse your brush, and paper towels for spills. You'll also often need a shirt board to hold your garment flat and stable as well as masking tape to attach the garment to the shirt board.

PAINTS AND DYES: While some of our projects don't call for paint, it's easiest to begin with this basic type of equipment. We use acrylic paints and acrylic fabric dyes. These are easy to work with on fabric and are nontoxic and safe to use at home.

Among the acrylic paints, we use several brands of dimensional paints. These are formulated for use on fabric and may be applied directly from the tube or bottle. The acrylic dyes we use are also meant for use on fabrics. You may wish to use artist's acrylic paints in a project; if so, pay close attention to the discussion below about textile medium. After being

Decorating your denims calls for a variety of paints; most are available in craft stores.

applied to fabric, acrylic dyes and artist's acrylic paints usually must be heat-set—either ironed or briefly placed in the dryer.

The dimensional paints and acrylic dyes we use come from several reputable companies, including Tulip Productions, Delta/Shiva, Galacraft, Inc., Duncan, and M. Grumbacher. The basic types of dimensional paint made by Tulip, Delta, and Galacraft include "slick," "iridescent," and "glitter." Slick paints—including Tulip Slick Paint, Delta Shiny Stuff for Fabric, and Galacraft Gala Color Plain—dry to a bright and slightly raised finish. Iridescent paints have a pearlized finish that is raised and shiny but slightly opaque, almost milky. Tulip Iridescent Fabric Paint, Delta Shiny Opalescent Fabric Paint, and Galacraft Gala Color Pearl are all iridescent paints. Glitter paint contains minuscule bits of glitter in a dimensional paint medium. Tulip Productions, Delta/Shiva, and Galacraft, Inc., all offer glitter paints. Duncan Scribbles Dimensionals provides slick,

iridescent, and glitter finishes and is widely available.

When you want a fancy look, Galacraft Crystal Gala Color and Tulip Candi Crystals contain coarse pieces of glitter that give a special sparkle. Another fashion look comes from Tulip Fiber Fun! Fashion Paint and Galacraft Galafetti, which contain tiny pieces of shredded foil in a clear or tinted medium. When using any glitter paint, be aware that the glitter that is loose and on the surface of the paint (i.e., not actually *within* the paint) will wash away the first time the garment is washed.

When a project calls for permanent fabric dyes, we use products by M. Grumbacher or Delta/Shiva. Delta/Shiva's Starlite and Grumbacher's Galaxy lines of fabric dyes are intended for use on dark colors, making them a good choice for denim. If you want to try a light-colored dye, you should work with it before using it on your garment.

When you use artist's acrylic paints to paint fabric, you'll need Delta/Shiva's Textile Medium.

This is a milky liquid that adapts these paints to fabric and helps them adhere to the fabric. It is usually spread on the fabric first; then the color is applied on top of the medium. Textile medium dries fast, so it's important to work quickly. Detailed directions for its use are on the bottle. When used with artist's acrylic paints, textile medium will leave a matte finish.

Each company makes many specialized products that we may choose for a particular project. In the directions for a project, we'll tell you what, if anything, can be substituted in that project. For example, Tulip Productions makes Jumpin' Jeans Denim Paint, which offers neon and regular colors for use on dark fabrics. You can find similar neon colors from other companies.

There are several tips we have learned that will be helpful. Some glitter and crystal paints take on a greenish cast when applied to dark denim colors. This doesn't happen with every color of every paint, but we've seen it often enough to consider the possibility in our designs. You should do the same in projects that call for such paints. Also, some colors that are brushed in may get "lost" on dark denim. Don't count on using pastel tints or a pale shade of crystal on a dark denim garment.

Fabric paints dry quickly. If you aren't applying paint directly from its container, place paint on your palette and immediately cap or close the paint container.

BRUSHES: Only a few specific brushes are used in this book, but you'll want to be able to substitute one brand for another if your selection is limited.

Brushes are available in either bristle or sponge. A sponge brush is a rectangle of fine-grain synthetic sponge that is angled at its tip; the bottom of the sponge is slit to fit onto a wooden stick. These brushes come in various widths.

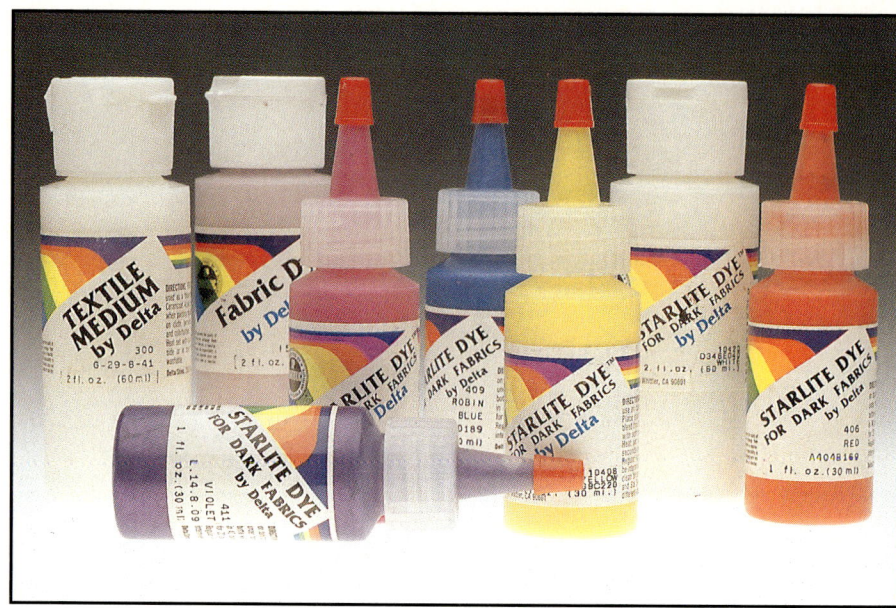

Various fabric dyes are used to decorate garments; these dyes are permanent and will not wash out if properly applied.

We use only a few brushes for our projects.

We use only 1-inch-wide and 2-inch-wide sponge brushes. Sponge brushes are inexpensive and easy to clean with water.

There's much greater variety in bristle brushes, which can be categorized by their size, width, and degree of bristle fineness.

Artist's brushes are classified by a numbering system—1 through 12. This will help you in choosing brush sizes when you buy from a manufacturer other than the one we mention in a particular project. Bristles can be either natural or synthetic. We find synthetic

For almost any denim you design, a variety of pens and pencils are used to sketch in designs at the beginning or to add details as you go along.

PENS AND PENCILS: When you need to sketch a design on denim, you'll usually use a pastel pencil. These pencils, which can be found in craft shops and artist's supply stores, produce a chalky line on a garment that can be gently brushed away when it is no longer needed. We use Conté à Paris pencils, which come in dozens of colors. For the projects in this book, you'll need only black to trace on light-colored denim and white to trace on dark-colored denim.

If you're working on a light-colored denim, you may want to use a pen with washable, or "disappearing," ink. This ink gives an easy-to-see line that fades away in a day or so. Some pens labeled "washable" hold ink that is actually permanent and stays even after washing. Look for a pen that specifically says its ink is disappearing.

Many crafters like to sign their work. On light-colored denim, you can use fabric pens by Marvy or Niji, which give an extremely fine line, to write an unobtrusive but permanent signature. On dark denim, try Tulip Slick Fine Line Paint Writer, or practice with a brush and slick or iridescent paint.

GLUE: Use only fabric glue to decorate clothing. Any other type of glue is likely to wash out, and your work will literally go down the drain. Many brands of fabric glue are available, but we use Slomons Stitchless Fabric Glue. Be sure to use a good amount of glue to set and hold any embellishments. The glue should cover the back and all edges of the embellishment.

CRAFT KNIFE: When we mention a craft knife, we mean a very small, very sharp blade on a handle. The most commonly used is the X-Acto, which has a pointed, single-edge blade in a long handle.

bristles fine for our purposes, and they're easy to clean. We use brushes from Liquitex and Tulip by Marx; Robert Simmons, Inc., M. Grumbacher, and Loew-Cornell, Inc. also make reliable brushes.

The bristle brushes we use most often are shaders, which have a chiseled edge that becomes sharper when wet. These brushes give a broad, flat line. If the edge of the brush is used as you apply paint, a shader gives a fine, thin line. Shaders come in "short" and "regular," but you can select them according to the number we give in each project.

Many beginning crafters use a paper cup to rinse and hold their brushes. If you do, be careful not to let the cup get top-heavy and spill. Try using a sturdy plastic cup instead of a paper cup. As you become more skillful and acquire more brushes, you may want to buy a brush bin. These plastic tubs, which may be round

or square, feature a divider that separates dirty brushes and water from clean. The bottom of the tub has brush rests on the "clean" side and ridges on the "dirty" side that help scrape paint off a brush. The rim of the bin offers holes to store brushes upright rather than flat. The cover of the bin makes a good palette.

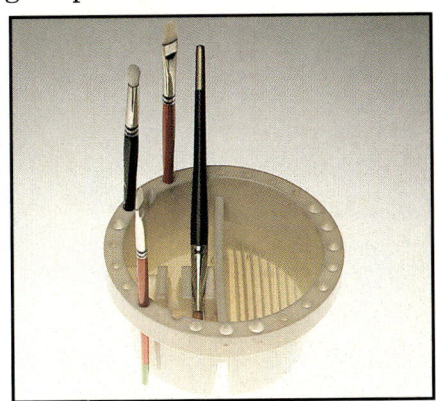

As you become more skilled, you may want to buy a brush bin to hold and clean your brushes.

ADHESIVE WEB: To attach fabric to fabric, you may use glue, dimensional paint, or adhesive web. Adhesive web is ironed onto a fabric and causes that fabric to adhere to another surface. Variety and craft stores carry many brands of adhesive web. Our favorite is Pellon Wonder-Under Transfer Web, which has adhesive web on one side and paper on the other. After you have ironed fabric onto the web side, place the fabric where you want it. You then remove the paper and iron the fabric on. All adhesive web products come with complete directions; always follow the manufacturer's instructions.

SHIRT BOARD: When painting fabric, you must keep the fabric flat, taut, and stable. You also need a surface under the fabric that won't absorb any paint that soaks through the fabric. Shirt boards are pieces of cardboard cut to about the size of a T-shirt that hold the garment. One side of the board is coated with wax and won't absorb paint. The shirt board we like best is Band a Board; another choice is Tee-Board.

It's possible to improvise your own shirt board. Get a piece of thick cardboard at least 24 inches by 20 inches in size. Trim it to fit your garment. Cover one side of the cardboard with wax paper (plastic wrap is too slippery) and use masking tape to securely fasten the wax paper to the cardboard. This can also work for children's garments, which are too small for standard shirt boards.

You can also make a custom board if you want to decorate the sleeves, neckline, shoulders, or bottom of a shirt or jacket. Locate the center of the area you wish to decorate. Measure the widest point at the center and then measure the length. Cut a piece of cardboard to fit the widest point and the entire length. Slip the cardboard into the garment

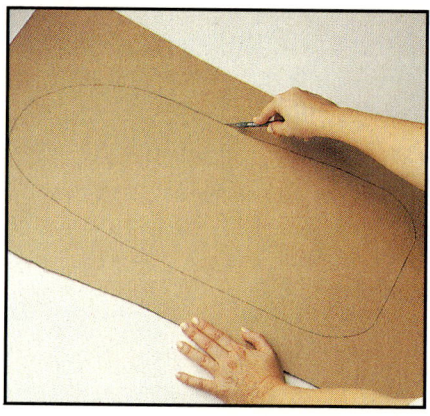 

You can make your own shirt board by cutting a piece of cardboard to a desired size and then taping wax paper on the cut piece of cardboard.

to make sure it fits reasonably well, then begin trimming to accommodate the smaller areas. When you've trimmed enough for a good fit, cover one side of the board with wax paper, using masking tape to hold it tight.

Choosing, Preparing, and Caring for Your Garments

Denim that's 100 percent cotton is the most common, and it gives the best decorating results. Denim that contains a small amount of synthetic fibers works well, too.

Always wash and dry a garment before decorating it. Starches, dirt, and whatever else the garment has picked up before reaching you must be removed or your decorating work may not properly adhere. Washing denim is important because cotton might shrink, even when it's prewashed. Use regular laundry detergent—not one containing fabric softeners. Dry your garment according to the garment's care label or in the dryer at medium heat to make sure the garment has shrunk as much as it's going to shrink. Don't use fabric softeners; they can affect the garment's surface and therefore your decorating.

After you've decorated a garment, you generally will be able to wash it in the washer. However, *never* wash a decorated garment until you've given it at least a week to set. Some of our design instructions say it's OK to wear a garment as soon as it's dry; wearing is fine, but washing is not. Paint and glue need a week to "cure," and they will suffer if you wash them too soon.

When a decorated garment is ready to wash, use a gentle or delicate setting and pure, mild soap (Ivory Snow or Dreft, for example). Other detergents—including those advertised for delicate hand-washables—contain "lifting" agents that will disturb your garment's decoration. Always use fabric softener with decorated denim, either in the final rinse cycle or when you fluff the garment in the dryer. Fabric softener keeps paint flexible.

Don't just toss your decorated denim in the dryer; take a few minutes to handle with care. Set the dryer to "air" and fluff your garment on this setting for a few minutes. If you skipped fabric softener in the wash, use a sheet-type softener now. After a few minutes in the dryer, remove the garment and let it dry on a line. A dryer's heat can cause your garment to shrink, or it may

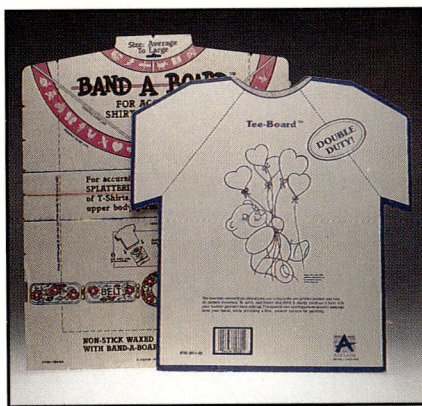

Ready-made shirt boards are available at many craft shops.

Thinking About Decorating

Once you've seen how easy and how fun it is to decorate your denims, you'll want to let your imagination soar. The techniques you'll learn can be easily adapted to other designs and fabrics. Your new skills will give you the chance to try something new.

You can start experimenting by taking another look at the "Tips and Variations" we've added to some of the designs. Thinking about those ideas can lead to a whole new interpretation of a design. Or you can take a design you like and think about how to carry it over to a different denim garment.

You can try working with colors other than those we suggest in a design; start with colors you like best. Color combinations, as with other design elements, work best in odd numbers—usually three or five. Consider working with a design that uses fabric along with paint. It's easier to get the colors you like in fabric and then affix the fabric to denim than it is to make the color come out exactly right when painted on your garment.

Feel free to think up your own designs. Designs can help bring out your figure's best points while downplaying its faults. For example, if you're short, decorating a coordinated outfit gives an elongating effect. Try trimming a skirt with horizontal rows of lace if you're slender; focus interest on shoulders or the hemline if you're not.

There are only two rules to remember when decorating your denims: The rules are made to be broken, and the work is meant to be fun. If you keep these two rules in mind, you'll always be happy with your work.

soften the paint so that it sticks to itself, resulting in a peeling and disappearing design. Even if the garment's manufacturer and the paint's manufacturer indicate machine washing and drying are safe, we believe it's safer and smarter to follow these guidelines.

Glitter Vest

With a shimmery sheen and colors that appear and disappear almost magically, Glitter Vest is one of those wonderful accessory garments that tops off any outfit. Glitter Vest will make you feel dressed up every time you wear it. But the very simplicity of Glitter Vest makes it appropriate for any age; even a toddler can enjoy its subtle interplay of light and color.

The simplicity of Glitter Vest also makes it a perfect choice for your first effort at fabric painting. Read through the directions several times; all you need are a few colors of paint and a brush, and you're in business. Glitter Vest is quick to finish, so you can decorate your vest in no time and wear it as soon as the paint is dry. The color of your vest will affect the final appearance of Glitter Vest. With a dark-colored vest, the various colors will show only when caught by light. A light-colored vest will give a different look—the colors will show easily and boldly. Remember that drying time depends on humidity—a muggy day can keep paint wet an extra 24 hours, while dry conditions may shorten drying time by several hours.

What You'll Need

- Denim vest; we used blue, but any color would work

- Glitter paint in at least five colors, to suggest a rainbow; we used Tulip Candi Crystals in lemon, spearmint, plum, neon pink, and icicle (white)

- Silver pencil for sketching; we used Berol Verithin No. 753

- Ruler

- Brush; we used a Liquitex No. 10 Nylon Flat shader

1. Prepare vest by washing, drying, and placing on a flat surface. Arrange paints to work from lightest to darkest colors. Next, using a silver pencil and ruler, sketch in lines to serve as guides when you are painting.

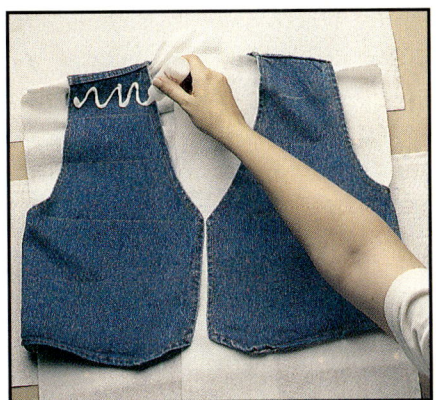

2. After all lines have been drawn, place paper towels in vest to prevent excess paint from flowing onto your work surface. Starting at the shoulder seam, squeeze a line of the lightest paint onto the right side of vest.

3. Dampen your brush; be sure to remove excess water from bristles, ferrule, and handle. Gently spread the paint on the vest with the brush. As soon as you finish the right side, repeat on the left side. Working with the same color from side to side keeps rainbow stripes aligned.

4. Continue to place paint on fabric and brush in. Gently blend each color with the bottom of the previous color's line. It's not necessary to wash brush when you change colors, and a bit of the previous color will help blend the shades together. If bristles begin to stiffen, rinse paint from brush and resume working. Continue to bring the colors across the entire width of the garment.

5. When you've finished painting the front, allow paint to dry (at least 12 hours). Turn the vest over to paint the back side, again placing paper towels. We chose to paint the back randomly, simply placing squiggles of paint on the fabric. Gently brush paints around and into each other. When you've finished painting the back of the vest, allow paint to dry (again, at least 12 hours).

Tips and Variations

You don't be need to be perfect. Glitter Vest allows shading and blending of colors, whether you're working with stripes or a random distribution of color. For an even easier project, use the random look on both the front and back.

Consider embellishing Glitter Vest by adding a three-dimensional aspect. Wait until paint is dry, then squiggle doodlelike lines and shapes onto the fabric straight from the tube. Allow these lines to dry without brushing them out.

Shredded 'n' Studded

Here's a project to vent your frustrations. You just can't stay mad when you're snipping away at a perfectly good pair of jeans. If you're really steamed, start poking holes in the fabric and see how fast your mood changes! You may be appalled at the idea of slashing, shredding, and otherwise damaging a brand-new pair of jeans. That's why we recommend using the oldest pair of jeans you can find. This look is popular with teenagers, though, and they grow fast. So, if you want to use a new pair of jeans, just wash them a few times before starting to work. The actual age of the garment doesn't matter; the idea is to make the jeans look virtually destroyed yet leave them sufficiently intact to be sure they'll last a long time. Although this is an easy project, read the directions through before starting.

What You'll Need

- Denim jeans, any color — the older, the better

- Ruler

- Pastel pencil in black; we used Conté à Paris

- Sharp scissors

- Heavy cardboard or a cardboard box

- Craft knife; we used an X-Acto

- Decorative studs; we used various shapes and sizes

- Flat-headed screwdriver

1.   Prepare jeans by washing and drying. Lay jeans flat, front side up. Place ruler across right leg and use pastel pencil to mark spots to be shredded; lines can be straight or angled. End each line at least one inch from the seams on either side. Shred marks should run down the right leg from mid-thigh to the bottom seam. Only the front will be shredded; the jeans would quickly fall apart if they were shredded front and back.

2.   When marking is complete, use scissors to cut along each line, working from the top to the bottom of the leg. Start from the inner side of the leg and work to the outer side.

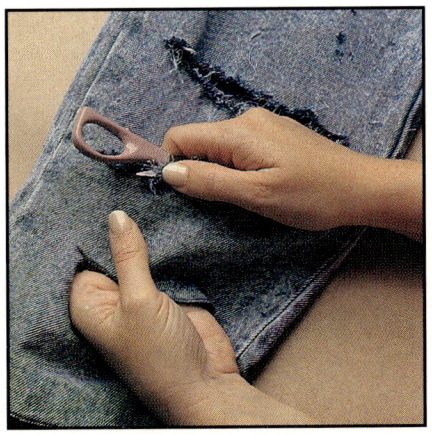

3.   To promote shredding, rub the blade edge of the scissors along the cut edges of the fabric.

 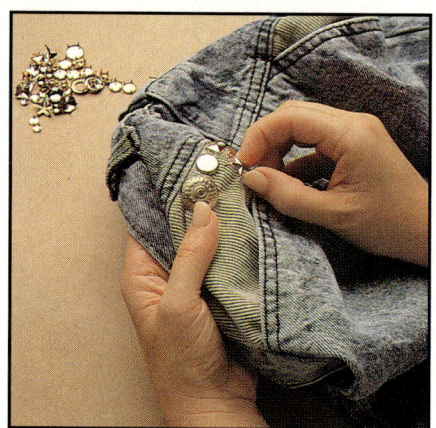 

4. To make holes in left leg, place jeans on top of heavy cardboard or a cardboard box (you'll be making a lot of holes in whatever is beneath the jeans). Hold the craft knife firmly and jab point into fabric. Repeat until you have the number of holes you want. Be sure to distribute holes randomly along the entire length of the left leg. Fray the holes with the scissors as done with the cuts in the right leg.

5. Now begin studding. Decide where you'll place studs, considering their sizes and shapes. Work with one stud at a time. To affix a stud to the jeans, place the stud at its chosen spot and press it into the fabric so that the prongs are visible on the underside of the fabric.

6. Expose the underside of the fabric and use the screwdriver to bend prongs under and inward. Repeat until all the studs are in place.

Tips and Variations

Although these jeans are likely to be worn with tights or leggings underneath, do remember they're a garment. Be careful in planning where holes and shredding end up.

To give your jeans a bit of color, use fabric paint to

draw circles around the holes you poked.

To continue the look, consider shredding a jacket or vest. Or just poke holes in a matching garment.

Dinosaur Dynasty

Here's a jacket for the child who's wild about dinosaurs! Dinosaur Dynasty is so easy you might consider allowing your young naturalist to work on the project on his or her own. If the painting and stamping seem too messy, let the youngster do the gluing.

What You'll Need

- Child's jean jacket

- Shirt board

- 2-inch sponge brush

- Dimensional fabric paint; we used Duncan Scribbles Dimensionals in red, blue, yellow, and green

- Palette (wax paper, paper plate, or top of a brush bin)

- Four precut sponges in dinosaur shapes, each sponge about five inches long

- Embellishments: pom-poms, "moving" eyes, plastic eyelashes, etc.

- Fabric glue; we used Slomons Stitchless Fabric Glue

1. Prepare jacket by washing, drying, and taping to shirt board to work on the back of the jacket. Dampen sponge brush and wring dry, leaving it slightly damp. Be sure to remove excess water from sponge and handle. Place a dollop of paint on palette and load brush with this color. Coat one dinosaur sponge lightly with the paint. Don't use too much paint; think of buttering toast.

2. Stamp sponge onto jacket twice.

3. Begin working with a second sponge and a second color. Use only one color per sponge. When changing colors, be sure to wash paint from brush. It's best to work with all four sponges and all four colors at once to be sure you have enough of each color and each shape. As you work, stamp dinosaurs to overlap, but not to cover each other. When you've stamped as many dinosaurs as you want on the back of the jacket, let the paint dry at least two hours. When the paint is dry, retape the jacket on the board to work on the front of the jacket. Repeat steps 1 through 3 on the jacket front.

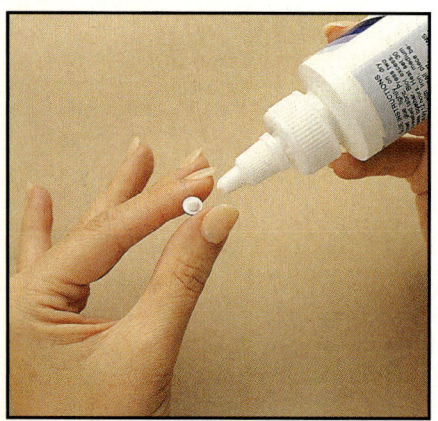

4. Choose a few of the most prominent, most clearly stamped dinosaurs (no more than three) to embellish. Place a dollop of fabric glue on a chosen embellishment.

5. Affix embellishments to dinosaurs. Allow the glue to dry before wearing the jacket.

Tips and Variations

Another approach to embellishing this jacket is to outline the most prominent shapes with dimensional paint straight from the tube.

For an adult, try a safari jacket on khaki, using the shapes of tigers, elephants, and giraffes.

Neon Jeans

Here's a fashion statement as bold as the neon bright colors splashed on a pair of jeans. It's so easy to create, you can feel free to let the child who will wear the jeans have a hand in decorating them. Read the instructions through a couple of times; you'll quickly recognize the points at which a child can take charge—especially spattering paint on the jeans. Neon Jeans is a fun style for preteens, but a younger child would enjoy this look, too. For a knockout outfit, take a look at our Sugar 'n' Spice jacket, which uses the same colors in a delightful design.

What You'll Need

- Denim jeans; stonewashed or prewashed are best

- Fluorescent fabric paint in three colors; we used Tulip Slick Paint in pink, yellow, and green

- Palette (wax paper, paper plate, or top of a brush bin)

- Shader brush; we used Tulip by Marx small flat shader

Tips and Variations

For a fancier look, add embellishments to your Neon Jeans. Consider gluing lace in neon-bright shades to pockets, cuffs, and/or side seams. You could add studs in amusing shapes, placing them along the painted seams. Try gluing on rhinestones in crystal or bright colors.

1.   Prepare jeans by washing and drying. Lay jeans flat and consider which seams and panels to paint in which colors. To begin painting, place a dollop of paint on palette. Dampen brush; wipe excess water from bristles, ferrule, and handle. Load brush with paint and start painting pocket inset.

2.   After painting both pocket insets, paint top yoke of jeans.

3.   Next, apply paint to loops, seams, zipper fly, and bottom seams directly from tube.

4.   Brush out paint so that loops, seams, and fly acquire a mottled look, rather than an even layer of color. When the paint is dry—about an hour— turn the jeans over and repeat on the back of the jeans.

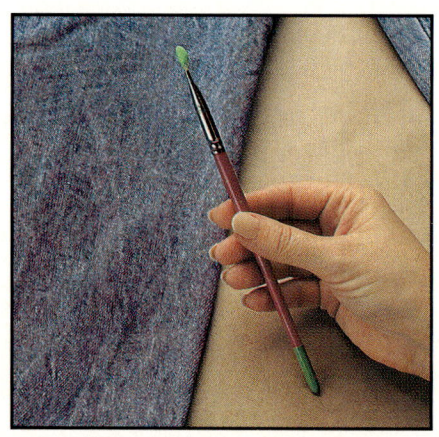

5.   When all paint has dried, you're ready to spatter. Place jeans flat, front side up, in an open area—outdoors, if possible, or in your basement or work area. The paint is likely to spatter beyond the jeans, so be sure to work in an area where this is permissible. Place a dollop of paint on palette and dampen brush. Load brush heavily with paint.

6.   Hold the brush about six inches above jeans and rap it sharply against the edge of your hand so that paint spatters down onto jeans. Repeat three or four times. Do the same with the second and third colors. Allow spattered paint to dry—about an hour—and turn jeans over to spatter back.

Charming Vest

Charming is just the word for this delightful and versatile concept. Charming Vest began as a Victorian-inspired array of charms and lace, buttons and bows, all attractively arranged and glued to a simple black vintage vest. Here, we've transferred the idea to denim to show you just how adaptable Charming Vest can be.

What You'll Need

- Denim vest; we used black, but other colors may work depending on the embellishments you use

- Shirt board

- Charms, acrylic gems, buttons, doily, cut-out fabric flowers or shapes (to make fabric yo-yos, see our design Victorian Lace), and other embellishments

- Fabric glue; we used Slomons Stitchless Fabric Glue

1.   Prepare vest by washing, drying, and taping to a shirt board. Assemble the embellishments you wish to use.

2.   Work with the charms in various ways to create a pleasing overall arrangement. If your vest has pockets, a collar, buttons, or other design elements, be sure to incorporate these into your arrangement.

3.   When you've arranged the embellishments to your satisfaction, you're ready to start gluing. Working with one embellishment at a time, place a dab of glue on the vest at the place the embellishment will go.

4.   Gently press embellishment to affix it to vest. If any excess glue shows, blot it immediately. If you're grouping embellishments, complete one group before moving to another area.

5.   After all embellishments have been glued on, allow glue to dry. Heat-set by ironing on the wrong side at medium heat for about 20 seconds.

Tips and Variations

Try Charming Vest on black velvet. Be very careful not to let excess glue seep out from under the embellishments.

Turn Charming Vest into a Lost in the Stars vest. Use a cascade of acrylic star-shaped rhinestones in varying colors, two star charms, a large airplane, and a gold bird.

Turn Charming Vest into a Key to My Heart vest. Use two gold heart charms, two gold heart lockets, one large and two small gold key charms, braid trim for the pockets, and acrylic heart-shaped rhinestones in varying colors and sizes.

Lamé and Lace

Make it today, wear it tonight. That's how easy this elegant Lamé and Lace project is. Our appliqué technique involves no sewing. About all you'll need is a ruler and lots of trim in varying textures to create this glittering gem of a vest. Once you've read through the directions a few times and visualized the process of making it, you'll want to try Lamé and Lace with other fabrics and different trim. The most important thing to remember as you work is keeping the diagonal lines on each side of the vest aligned so they'll meet when your vest is buttoned.

Lamé and Lace

What You'll Need

- Denim vest; we used black, but white would work

- Shirt board

- Ruler

- Pastel pencil in white; we used Conté à Paris

- One spool (about one yard) gold sequinned braid

- One spool (about one yard) gold metallic rickrack, 1 inch wide

- One yard black braid

- One yard gold and black flat braid

- One yard gold lace

- Fabric glue; we used Slomons Stitchless Fabric Glue

- Sharp scissors

- One yard gold lamé ruffle

1.   Prepare vest by washing, drying, and taping to shirt board. Work with the vest buttoned to keep the trim aligned on each side. Using ruler and pastel pencil, draw lines to guide where trim will go. Starting at arm side of sleeve hole, draw an angled line with pastel pencil across vest to neck side of vest.

2.   Work downward from the first line, drawing parallel lines on one side of vest until reaching the buttons. Space the lines about two inches apart. Once one side is finished, repeat the process on the other side. As you work, be careful to keep the lines aligned so they will meet at the middle in the shape of the letter V. Continue to make lines to the bottom of the vest.

3.   Now arrange the pattern of decorations you'll affix to the vest. Use every trim except the gold lamé ruffle. Arrange the trim in different orders, working until you like the arrangement. After you've decided where you want each type of trim to go, you're ready to glue. But don't glue anything until you've decided the final arrangement.

4.   To fasten the trim onto the vest, work on one side of the vest at a time. Work on one row at a time, starting from the top. Place a line of glue on the pencil line for the row.

5. Place a line of trim on the glue. Press to spread the glue and affix the trim firmly to vest. If you used too much glue, blot excess glue and use a little less on the next line.

6. After all gluing is done, cut the trim from its length, using a sharp scissors for a clean cut. Repeat steps 4 through 6 to finish the other side of the vest.

7. To decorate the vest neckline, keep the vest buttoned. Place a line of glue, starting from the buttoned end on the buttonhole side and moving up and around the neckline to about the center of the back. Place gold lamé ruffle along this glue, pressing gently to affix to the vest. Now glue from mid-back down the other side of the vest neckline.

8. Place ruffle along this line of glue, again pressing gently to affix to vest. When all glue is dry, heat-set either by ironing vest on the wrong side at medium heat for about 20 seconds or by placing in a dryer at medium setting for about 10 minutes.

Tips and Variations

For a dramatic evening outfit, try this design on a black velvet vest worn with velvet pants over a black turtleneck. Or try it on other fabrics, such as satin or a smooth gabardine.

If you prefer silver to gold, try Lamé and Lace in an all-silver motif.

Gem Explosion

The teenager who wears Gem Explosion could be a rock star—in more ways than one. It's hard to say what's more stunning about Gem Explosion: the extraordinarily striking three-dimensional look or the amazing ease with which it's created. Once you've read the directions through a couple of times, you'll see that the hardest step in executing this incredible jacket is arranging the gems on the white background. That task took us about an hour. Otherwise, Gem Explosion is a simple and quick matter of painting, spreading, and sticking.

What You'll Need

- Denim jacket; we used bleached blue, but black or white would also work

- Shirt board

- 10-inch dinner plate

- Pastel pencil in black; we used Conté à Paris

- Iridescent fabric paint; we used Tulip Iridescent Fabric Paint in turquoise

- Glitter paint; we used Tulip Liquid Glitter in silver

- Plastic fork

- Gems; we used about 80 aurora borealis light blue sapphires 15 to 20 millimeters in size and in varying shapes by Puttin' on the Glitz

1. Prepare jacket by washing and drying. Tape jacket to a shirt board with the back of the jacket resting on the wax side of the board. Center plate on the back of the jacket. Using pastel pencil, trace around plate. Remove plate.

2. To make back of jacket taut for painting, tape pleat with masking tape.

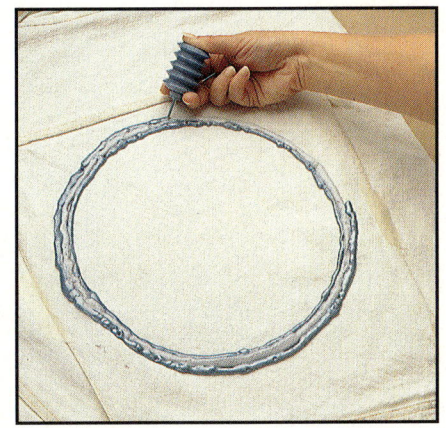

3. Using the circle as a guide, draw three concentric circles with alternating paints: first turquoise, then silver glitter, then turquoise again. The innermost circle is the one following the line left by the plate. These rings of color should be about the thickness of a pencil and rest immediately next to each other.

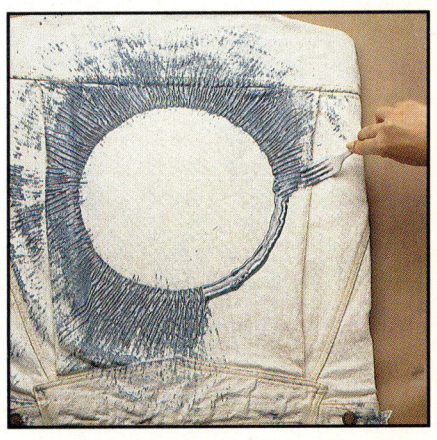

4. Remove masking tape. Using plastic fork, draw paint away from the center in jagged lines of varying lengths for an "explosion" effect. Lines should be thick enough to give a three-dimensional effect.

5. Fill in unpainted center area with gems, arranging them until you like the overall design. Don't be too precise; mix sizes and shapes for a random "explosion" look.

6. When you're satisfied with the arrangement, begin affixing the gems. Working with one gem at a time, pick up a gem and paint its flat side with plenty of silver glitter paint. Return each gem to its place. Continue until entire circle is filled, and all gems are affixed.

7. Now look over the circle, filling in any open spots with silver glitter paint. No denim should show through. As you work, check every edge of every gem to be sure it is firmly secured to the jacket.

8. Frame the area containing the stones with a thick line of silver glitter paint. After the paint is dry, turn the jacket over and fill in right pocket with gems and silver glitter paint as in steps 6 through 8.

Tips and Variations

Gem Explosion can have a completely different look if it's done with small mirrors or multicolored gems. Be sure to mix sizes and shapes for the effect that makes this jacket unique.

If you're really ambitious, try creating a pattern within the gemstones, perhaps layers of color or whatever else your imagination may suggest.

Navajo Sunset

Simple in design and as stunning as dusk in the West, Navajo Sunset's effect comes from the deep hues and subtle shadings that characterize nature's own sunsets. Although there is an abundance of shading, this project is easy enough for a beginner with time and patience. Read the directions a couple of times. It's wise to practice the shading technique that produces Navajo Sunset's imperceptible blending of color into color. For a stunning sunset look, you'll need plenty of paint in strong colors. The highest point in the sky is black, with purple, blue, red, and orange—in that order—underneath. The mountains are blackish-brown, and the sun is a blazing yellow.

What You'll Need

- **Denim jacket; we used black, but blue would work**

- **Shirt board**

- **Pastel pencil in white; we used Conté à Paris**

- **Textile medium; we used Textile Medium from Delta**

- **Brush; we used Liquitex No. 10 Nylon Flat shader**

- **Permanent fabric dyes: we used Delta Starlite Dye in black, brown, yellow, orange, red, blue, and purple**

- **Palette (wax paper, paper plate, or top of a brush bin)**

1. Prepare jacket by washing, drying, and taping to a shirt board. Decide whether you'll end the design at the horizontal shoulder seam, or carry it to the neckline. Using a pastel pencil, sketch freehand the outline of a design: three mountains with the sun partially visible in the crook of the two farther, higher mountains. Above the mountains sketch a set of four wavy lines across the back of the jacket. These lines will be a guide for placement of the colors of the sunset. Each section should be about three inches deep except the bottom section, which will be partially taken up by the mountains and sun.

2. After sketching in all lines, start working with the black mountain (the smallest) at the bottom of the jacket. First apply textile medium, following the directions on the bottle. Then begin filling in the black mountain. Dampen shader brush, being careful to wipe away any excess water from brush, ferrule, and handle. Place plenty of black dye on palette and load brush. Apply dye to top edge of black mountain and brush downward.

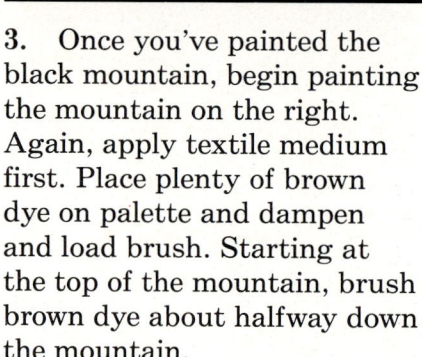

3. Once you've painted the black mountain, begin painting the mountain on the right. Again, apply textile medium first. Place plenty of brown dye on palette and dampen and load brush. Starting at the top of the mountain, brush brown dye about halfway down the mountain.

4.   Next, place black dye on palette and load brush. Do not rinse brush before loading with black dye. Stroke black upward and brown downward to blend the two colors. Finally, paint the mountain on the left. Apply textile medium and then paint in brown dye only.

5.   After you've finished painting in the mountains, you're ready to paint the sun. After applying textile medium, place yellow dye on palette. Dampen and load brush. Fill in the sun, working carefully to keep the yellow area defined from the surrounding colors.

6.   When the sun is finished, paint the sections of the sky. Apply textile medium before painting. Place plenty of orange dye on palette and dampen and load brush. Apply orange dye nearest to sun. While filling in orange around the sun, place a small dollop of yellow dye on palette and work in this touch of yellow to lighten the orange area near the sun. Bring orange dye down around the mountain shapes. As the orange section fills in, place red dye on palette and begin to apply red dye without rinsing brush. Blend red and orange dyes, stroking orange upward and red downward and leaving no visible lines to separate colors. Bring orange no more than a half inch into red section.

7.   As each section begins to fill in, start blending in the next color, working up the back of the jacket. Don't rinse brush when you change colors. When all painting is finished, allow plenty of time for dye to dry. After dye is completely dry, heat-set it either by ironing on the wrong side of fabric at a medium heat for about 20 seconds or by placing jacket in a dryer at medium setting for about 10 minutes.

Tips and Variations

Practice shading on an old piece of fabric before working on your jacket. Don't let one color go too far into its neighbor's space; this will give an uneven look.

If all the shading seems overwhelming, try the opposite approach: work *with bold stripes of color with no shading. You may like the look just as much as the shaded look.*

To highlight your the scene, add a touch of glitter paint to the mountaintops, or add cacti or small trees to the mountainside.

What preteen or teenage girl wouldn't love this jazzy jacket? It looks fabulous on its own, and also makes a terrific partner with Neon Jeans. If your little fashion plate is interested in learning about crafting, here's the chance to let her get some practice in. A child can apply paint from the tube or help glue embellishments. Acrylic paints are nontoxic, so you can feel safe while you enjoy this project together. Set a good example by reading through the directions a couple of times.

What You'll Need

- Girl's denim jacket

- Shirt board

- Pastel pencil in black; we used Conté à Paris

- Small plate; we used a teacup-size saucer

- Three pairs of plastic charm sunglasses in neon bright colors and three pairs of plastic charm red lips; we used the large size of lips and sunglasses by Jazz-Ups

- Three crystal rhinestones, about 13 millimeters; we used rhinestones from Puttin' on the Glitz

- Fluorescent fabric paints; we used Tulip Slick Paint in green, pink, and yellow

- Brush; we used Tulip by Marx small flat shader

- Fabric glue; we used Slomons Stitchless Fabric Glue

- Sharp scissors

- One yard of satin double-face ribbon, ⅛ inch wide, in a neon bright color; we used pink

- Palette (wax paper, paper plate, or top of a brush bin)

- One yard of lace in a neon bright color; we used chartreuse

1. Prepare jacket by washing, drying, and taping to a shirt board. The back of the jacket should be taped to the wax side of the board. Using pastel pencil and small plate, sketch the placement of three heads: the top head toward the left, the middle head toward the right, and the bottom head approximately centered. These circles will form the outline for each head. The size of the jacket will determine the distance between the heads, but they should be fairly close together.

2.   To get an idea of how the faces will look on the jacket and to gain perspective for sketching each girl's hair, place embellishments for each head. Lips go at the bottom of each circle, rhinestones serve as noses, and sunglasses go above. Don't glue yet.

3.   With embellishments in place, use pastel pencil to sketch in hair.

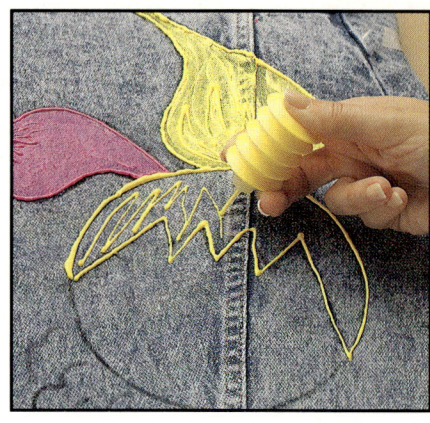

4.   Remove embellishments. Apply paint straight from the tube to hair, using a different color for each head.

5.   Dampen brush, removing excess water from bristles, ferrule, and handle. Brush out some of the paint to fill in empty spots. Allow about two hours for the paint to dry.

6.   When the paint is dry, put fabric glue on the sunglasses, rhinestones, and lips. Affix the embellishments in their places on the jacket.

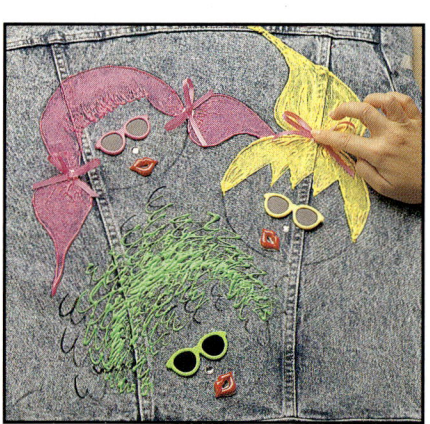

7.   Cut ribbon into three pieces of roughly equal length. Tie a small bow with each piece of ribbon. Affix these to hair with fabric glue: two on the pigtails, one on the ponytail.

8. Next, place a dollop of paint of each color on palette. Brush paint on top seam and bottom panel of the jacket. Use a different color for each seam: We used green for the top seam, yellow for the bottom flaps, and pink for the bottom panel. Allow the paint to dry. Remove the jacket from the board and retape so the front of the jacket is on the wax side of the board. Paint front seams, pockets, and panels in the same manner.

9. Remove the jacket from the board after all paint has dried. Trim collar and cuffs with lace, starting with the collar. Place a line of glue from one side of the collar to the other side.

10. Run lace along the glue to attach the lace to the collar. Blot any excess glue. Snip excess lace.

11. Repeat the process for the cuffs. Attach the lace to the top seam of the cuffs so it won't touch hands. This will help keep the lace reasonably clean.

Tips and Variations

Rather than painting the front seams, pockets, and panels, try putting one small face on the front, perhaps on a pocket.

For a more elaborate jacket, use more embellishments: *extra lace in different colors, more bows in different colors, tiny round mirrors, etc.*

Consider changing the hairdos of all three girls to match the hairdo of the girl who will wear the jacket.

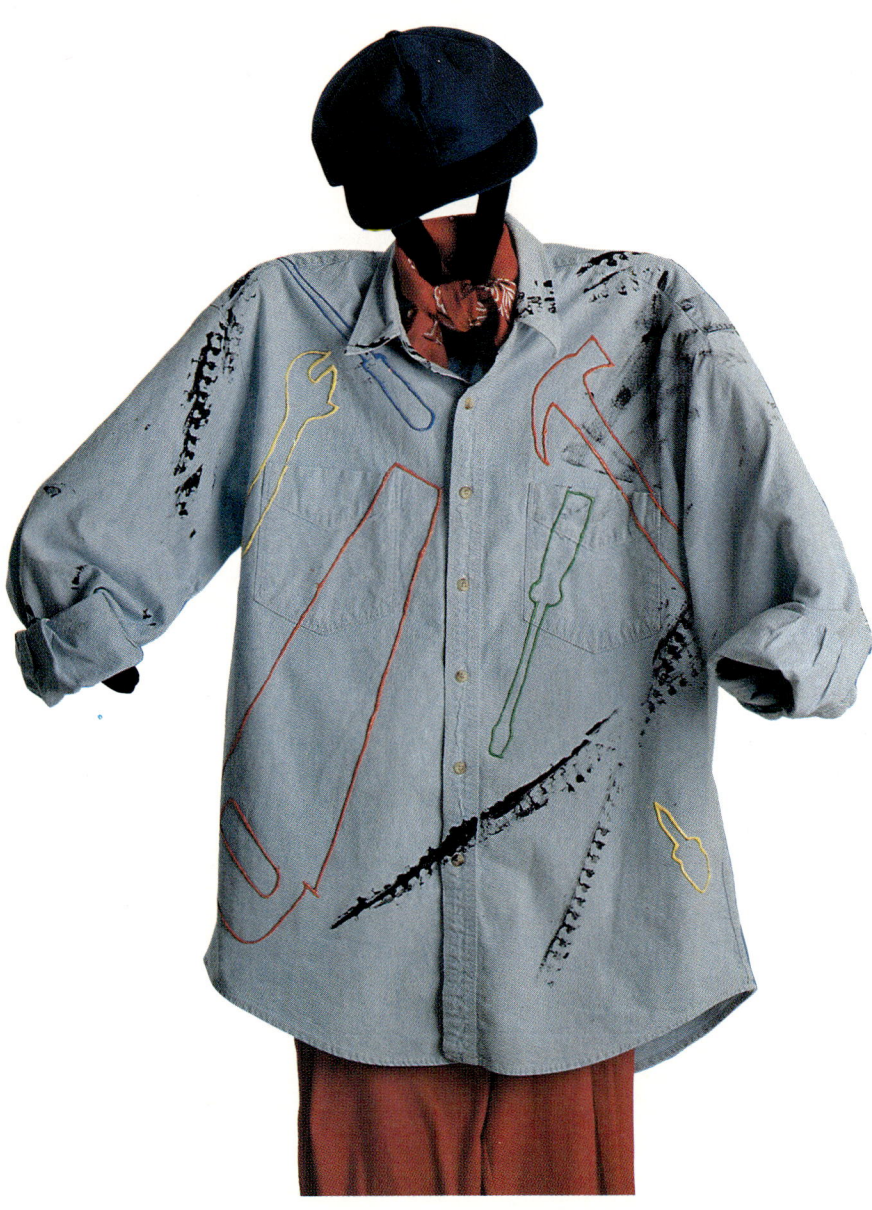

The handyman with a sense of humor will get a terrific laugh from this lighthearted commentary on the trusty old workshirt. You may be startled by the tire tracks, but reading the directions a couple of times will show you how easily they're made. If you have children, let them watch or they'll never believe you actually did it!

When you're selecting tools to outline on this shirt, place all the tools you want to use on the shirt at the same time; this will help you compare their relative sizes. If the shirt is too small to accommodate everything, consider using smaller versions of the tools—for example, a little screwdriver instead of the big one that most people really use. Or trace toy versions of the tools.

What You'll Need

- **Denim workshirt; we used blue**

- **Permanent fabric dye; we used Delta Fabric Dye in black**

- **Palette (wax paper, paper plate, or top of a brush bin)**

- **Bicycle tire**

- **2-inch sponge brush**

- **Shirt board**

- **Tools, such as hammer, screwdriver, wrench, etc.**

- **Pastel pencil in black; we used Conté à Paris**

- **Slick fabric paint; we used Duncan Scribbles Dimensionals in red, blue, green, and yellow**

- **Sharp scissors**

1.   Prepare shirt by washing and drying. Take shirt, fabric dye, palette, and bicycle tire outdoors or into your garage or basement. Place black fabric dye on palette. Run bicycle tire over palette, getting enough dye on the tire so treads will show when it runs over shirt.

2.   Carefully run dye-covered portion of the tire over the shirt near one arm, holding the shirt straight to make the tire mark clear. Repeat to make two more tire marks, one near the collar and one near the bottom of the shirt.

3.   Dampen sponge brush and squeeze almost dry, removing excess water from sponge and handle. Load brush with dye remaining on palette and spread it onto your hand.

4.   Blot dye onto the shirt, smearing to make a hand print that looks as if you had wiped a dirty hand on the shirt. If there's more dye left, spread it onto your hand and scrunch up handfuls of fabric to create "dirt" marks. Wash hands. After dye has dried—about an hour—heat-set either by ironing shirt on the wrong side at medium heat for about 20 seconds or by placing in dryer at medium setting for about 10 minutes.

5. Tape the shirt to the shirt board. Place the tools you want to trace on the shirt, working out a pleasant, random arrangement. Use a pastel pencil to trace each tool.

6. Remove traced tool and repeat with each tool, one at a time.

7. Working with slick paint straight from the tube, color the outline of each tool with a different color.

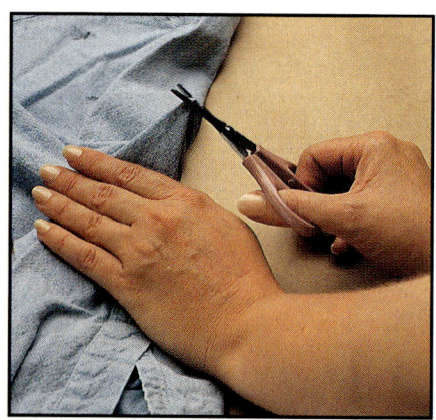

8. When the paint is dry, remove the shirt from the shirt board. Gather the fabric of one sleeve at the elbow and use sharp scissors to snip a small hole. Rub the cut edges together to begin fraying.

Tips and Variations

If you want to decorate the back of this shirt, remember to add another tire track and/or "dirt" marks. If you leave hand prints on the back of the shirt, why not put them where they usually would be—at the bottom of the back?

This shirt is wonderful for a child who loves tools. Collect some child-size tools to trace. Skip making the hole at the elbow—a child is likely to complete that step through everyday wear!

This is definitely not a serious shirt; feel free to have fun with it.

Whether you're heading for a square dance or the company picnic, Swing Your Partner brings a cheerful attitude everywhere. A pretty white blouse makes this a terrific outfit for any casual occasion. Swing Your Partner is a super-easy project. Measure a few lines, do a little gluing and you're ready to step out. Be sure to read the directions at least twice before setting to work; you will want to measure accurately to get just the right look. As you read, think about variations you might like to try. We thought of a fistful and we're sure you will, too.

What You'll Need

- **Full denim skirt with gathered yoke; we used black, but any basic denim would work**

- **Print fabric, about 36 inches by 45 inches, cut into enough 5-inch-wide strips to cover the circumference of the skirt; we used a gingham check print in red and white**

- **About ten yards of white lace, three inches deep, gathered for ruffling**

- **Ruler**

- **Pastel pencil in white; we used Conté à Paris**

- **Fabric glue; we used Slomons Stitchless Fabric Glue**

- **1-inch sponge brush**

- **Sharp scissors**

- **Braid trim, enough to cover the circumference of your skirt**

- **Round fabric doily in white**

1.   Wash skirt and gingham fabric. Place skirt on a large, flat surface. Measure width of lace. Then use a ruler to measure where the first row of lace will be attached to the skirt. The first row of lace should be attached so that the lace will extend one inch below the skirt's hemline. Using a pastel pencil, mark the point where lace should be attached.

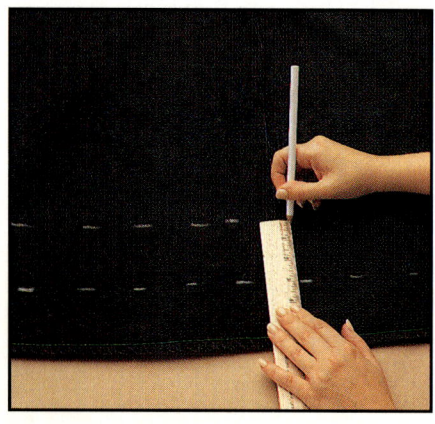

2.   Starting from the point where the first row of lace will be attached, measure up to find where the second row of lace should be attached. The second row of lace should extend far enough down to just cover the ruffle casing of the first row. Using a pastel pencil, mark that point around the circumference of the skirt. Repeat for the third row of lace.

3.   Now measure where the gingham fabric will go. Starting from the top of the third row of lace, measure to a point 5 inches above. Using a pastel pencil, mark this point around the skirt.

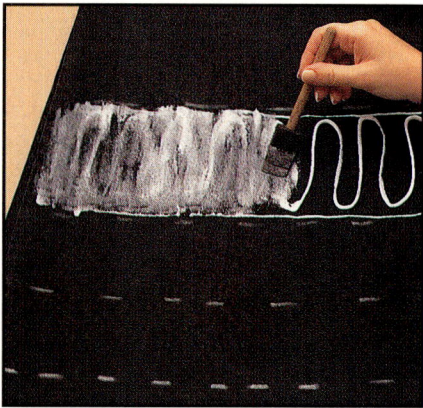

4.   Place fabric glue on the skirt in the area where the gingham fabric will be affixed. Dampen sponge brush; be careful to remove any excess water from the sponge and handle. Use brush to evenly spread the glue around.

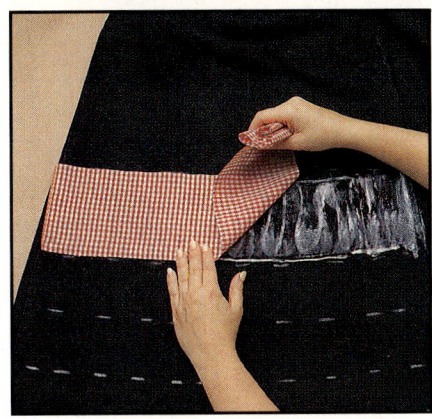

5.   Affix the gingham fabric on the glued area and smooth it down to work out any wrinkles or bubbles. Repeat, attaching additional strips of gingham around the circumference of the skirt.

6.   Using sharp scissors, cut three pieces of lace long enough to fit around the circumference of the skirt. Place a line of fabric glue at the bottom of the gingham fabric. Now place a row of lace at the bottom of the gingham fabric, attaching the lace's ruffle casing to the glue. Press and smooth lace, blotting any excess glue.

7.   Glue and attach second (middle) and first (bottom) rows of lace. Your line of glue should follow the points you marked earlier.

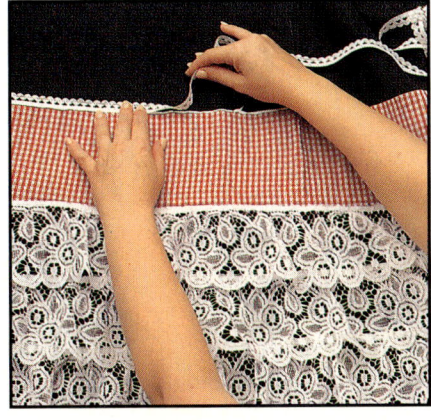

8.   Place a line of fabric glue at the top of the gingham fabric. Attach braid trim to the top of the gingham fabric, pressing to affix the braid to the fabric. Blot any excess glue.

9.   Decorate the skirt's pockets with fabric doily. Cut a round doily in half. Glue one half to each pocket with the straight side glued inside the top of the pocket. Then glue the round edge of the doily to the skirt. When all glue has dried, heat-set glue either by ironing on the wrong side at medium heat for about 20 seconds or by placing in a dryer set at medium setting for about 10 minutes.

Tips and Variations

Instead of gingham fabric, try a floral cotton in soft pastels. Get a totally different look by adapting Swing Your Partner to a black miniskirt. Trim with rows of gold lace, gold lamé, and/or black lace, running rows all the way up to the skirt's waistband.

Consider using the doily technique of step 9 on the skirt itself. Try running a row of doilies around the skirt and then punching out the denim behind the doilies. Wear a petticoat with the skirt for a wonderfully festive effect.

Try different trims on the skirt—cord, fringe, pom-poms—to give your skirt variety.

Jammin' Jumper

Wear Jammin' Jumper and you won't have to do a thing to whistle a happy tune! This is the perfect outfit for an informal dance, and it would be a hit at a square dance. It's a fun look for anyone who likes music, and that's just about everyone.

As you read through the directions for Jammin' Jumper, you may be concerned about trying to make the notes carry a tune. If you know music and would like to draw a few notes of a favorite melody, that's fine. But writing actual music is certainly not essential to an attractive design. Of real concern is keeping the lines of each staff straight and parallel with equal spacing. Also, be sure to distribute the staffs and the notes evenly. Avoid a crowded look in this design.

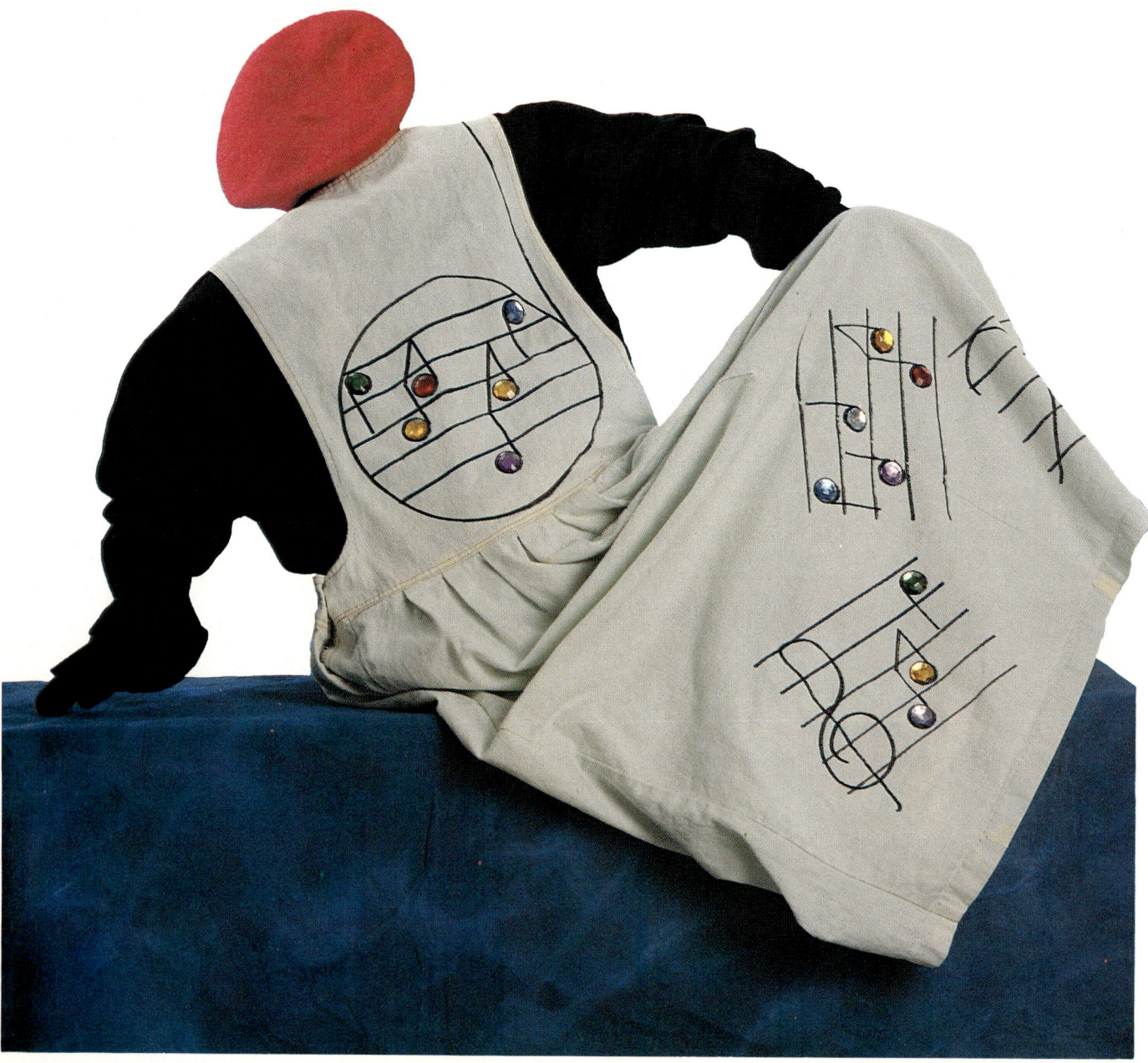

What You'll Need

- Denim jumper or dress with a flared skirt—the wider the flare the better—and an upper back large enough to center a dinner plate without touching the seams

- Shirt board

- Disappearing-ink pen

- Ruler

- Acrylic rhinestones, 22 millimeter size; we used Westrim Crafts in multicolors

- Permanent fabric marker; we used Fabric Painter by Speedball in black

- Slick fabric paint; we used Tulip Slick Paint in black

- 10-inch dinner plate

1.   Prepare dress by washing, drying, and taping front of skirt portion of dress to a shirt board. You'll probably be able to work on only one section of the skirt portion at a time. If so, make sure to allow plenty of time for each section to dry (at least a couple of hours) before you detach it and move to the next section. Working with disappearing-ink pen and ruler, sketch three staffs (a larger skirt may need more). Place ruler where you'll want the bottom line of the staff and draw along the ruler. Draw a total of five lines for each staff. Staffs should be angled to each other and spaced to give a random look. Each staff should be about 8 inches long and about 6 inches high.

2.   Using the disappearing-ink pen, draw a bass clef for one of the staffs. To make a bass clef, draw a line that looks somewhat like a backward letter C at the left side of the staff. Make this line large enough to extend from the top of the staff to below the bottom of the staff. Place one dot on the second line from the top and one dot on the middle line.

3.   Again using the disappearing-ink pen, make a treble clef on another staff. Draw a vertical line from below the bottom of the staff to the top of the staff. From the top of the line, draw a curve to resemble the letter P. Bring the curve down far enough to contain the top two spaces of the staff.

43

4. Bring the curve around behind the vertical line to make an upside-down, backward letter P. Bring the curve down far enough to contain the bottom two spaces of the staff.

5. Bring the bottom of the second P curve up and to the front of the vertical line to form a third curve opposite the second letter P. This last curve should also extend slightly behind the vertical line into a final curl.

6. Now decide where to place notes within each staff. There should be no more than five notes within each staff, and they should be distributed over the entire length of the staff. Place (but don't glue) a rhinestone—which will form the body of the note—for each note, making a pleasant arrangement with complementary colors.

7. Using the ruler and disappearing-ink pen, draw a stem for each note. Each stem should be about 2 to 2½ inches high.

8. Remove the rhinestones. Working with one staff at a time, use black permanent fabric marker to go over staff lines, stems of notes, and clefs.

9. Next, working with one rhinestone at a time, coat the back of the rhinestone with black slick fabric paint directly from the tube. Return the rhinestone to its place on the staff, pressing to affix. The fabric paint will act as glue. Repeat until all stones are in place, working with one staff at a time. Allow skirt to dry thoroughly, at least two hours.

10.   Now decorate the top of the garment. Tape the back section of the top to the shirt board. Place dinner plate on the dress just above the skirt seam and with equal spacing on the two sides. Using disappearing-ink pen, outline the plate and remove it from the garment.

11.   Make a staff of five lines within the circle. Using disappearing-ink pen, draw the middle line first and then draw two equally spaced lines above and below the middle line. Mark notes and stems as in steps 6 and 7.

12.   Now draw a stem off the main circle using disappearing-ink pen. Place the ruler's bottom next to the center line of the staff and draw a line of about 12 inches in length.

13.   Using permanent fabric marker, mark the staff and stems inside the large note, the body of large note, and the stem of the large note.

14.   Using black slick paint, affix rhinestones to staff as in step 9. Allow at least two hours for marker and paint to dry before removing dress from shirt board.

Tips and Variations

Consider Jammin' Jumper for a skirt-and-blouse outfit. The design would be just as charming on separates in other fabrics. Remember to choose a skirt with enough flare to show off the design.

If you'd like to continue the design on the front of the dress, try a tiny staff on the pocket flaps or a few randomly scattered notes.

Once you've become handy with the slick fabric paint, try painting over everything we did in permanent marker with slick paint. You'll like the high-gloss, three-dimensional effect slick paint gives the design.

Silk Flower Bouquet

Ever wish you had the perfect corsage—one that holds your favorite flowers and never wilts? Here it is, on an informal jacket that suggests a little smile about the silk flowers themselves. Silk Flower Bouquet is a pretty, feminine look but not a completely serious one. So try some fanciful colors and enjoy creating your own personal nosegay. The silk flowers require some special treatment to keep their shape, so be sure to read the directions thoroughly two or three times before starting. Since the bouquet will remain in the arrangement you give it, give yourself plenty of time to work carefully on the bouquet's design. Remember to always give this garment delicate treatment: Hand-wash it with a gentle soap such as Ivory Snow or Dreft, and fluff it in the dryer with fabric softener before hanging to dry.

What You'll Need

- **Denim jacket; bleached or stonewashed is best**

- **Shirt board**

- **Silk flowers in various colors and sizes, two stems of each; we used two large yellow roses and several smaller bluebells and pink tiger lilies**

- **Pastel pencil in black; we used Conté à Paris**

- **1-inch sponge brush**

- **Silk flower preservative; we used Dusty Pilot's Floraguard**

- **Fabric glue; we used Slomons Stitchless Fabric Glue**

- **Rhinestones, 9 millimeter and 15 millimeter**

- **Glitter paint; we used Tulip Glitter Pen in green**

- **Sharp scissors**

- **Double-face satin ribbon, ⅛ inch wide**

1. Prepare jacket by washing, drying, and taping to a shirt board. Set aside. Working with one flower at a time, separate flower blooms from stems. Set stems aside.

2. Working with all the flowers, create an arrangement on the jacket. Group flowers closely without crowding them. Keep one or two large blooms as the focal point, filling out the arrangement around them. The blooms should not extend beyond the shoulder or creep down the sleeve.

3. When you're happy with the arrangement, remove one bloom at a time and use a pastel pencil to mark the flower's place.

4. Working with one bloom at a time, gently separate layers to take flower apart. Discard the plastic center of the flower.

5. Dampen sponge brush, being careful to wipe excess water from sponge and handle. Following manufacturer's instructions, use the sponge brush to coat each flower layer with silk flower preservative. Allow flowers to dry (one to two hours).

6. Now return each flower to its place on the jacket. Work with one flower at a time, starting with the largest (focal point) flower. Place a dab of fabric glue on the jacket at the spot the largest flower will go. Affix the bottom layer of the flower to the jacket, pressing gently. Build up the flower layer by layer: Place a dab of fabric glue in the center of the previous layer and affix a new layer.

7. When you've finished reassembling the flower, place a dab of fabric glue in the flower's center and affix a 15 millimeter rhinestone. Repeat steps 6 and 7 to reassemble each flower, working with only one flower at a time. Use smaller rhinestones for smaller flowers.

8. Allow the glue to dry. To heat-set the glue, turn a hand-held hair dryer to its highest setting and blow it onto glued area for about 15 seconds. After the glue is set, sketch the stems for the bouquet, using a pastel pencil. Three to five stems is enough. Bring the stems down below the flowers about one-third the length of the bouquet.

9. Paint the sketched stems using green glitter paint straight from the tube.

10. Take several large leaves from the stems set aside in step 1 and decide where they would look best with the bouquet. Outline the leaves using a pastel pencil.

11. Paint the outline of the leaves, using green glitter paint straight from the tube. Add interest by sketching in a few leaf veins.

12. Now decorate the bouquet with ribbon. Using sharp scissors, cut the ribbon into several pieces. Tie all the pieces together and then tie a bow. Position the bow near the bouquet to your satisfaction. Fasten the bow to the jacket by placing a dab of fabric glue on the jacket and gently pressing the bow to affix it to the jacket. Blot away any excess glue.

Tips and Variations

If you can't find silk flower preservative, you can use permanent fabric dye to treat the flowers. Use fabric dye in colors that coordinate with your flowers. Separate flowers as in step 4 above. Place a little fabric dye on palette and brush onto the flowers with a dampened sponge brush. After gluing flowers to jacket, heat-set dye using a handheld hair dryer on its highest setting for about 20 seconds per flower.

To brighten your bouquet, use colored gems as flower centers.

Consider using this bouquet on a denim shirt or a cotton knit sweater. Be careful not to assemble a bouquet that's too heavy for the fabric.

Southwestern Duster

Southwestern Duster is a stunning duster that fashion magazines call "investment dressing"—an expensive but beloved and versatile garment you'll wear forever. You'll be happy to have it. Since you're making the garment yourself, your cost will be only a fraction of the hefty price tag you'd pay in a store. Just as delightful as the custom look you'll get in Southwestern Duster is the ease with which you'll create it. The only technique used here is gluing. The most complicated part is making the stars that decorate the duster. Read through the directions several times, and you'll see just how simple it is to create your own "investment dressing."

Tips and Variations

We also placed pieces of chamois on the front shoulders, trimming and gluing as shown. We placed one concha on the front at the left shoulder and added a smaller star on the right side in the front where the chamois wrapped around from the back of the duster.

Think about embellishments other than conchas you might want to add: pony beads, feathers, etc. If you'd like to be even more creative, consider different patterns for the star piece.

What You'll Need

- Denim duster; we used black, but blue would also work

- Five pieces of suede fabric, about 18 inches by 45 inches, each piece a different color; we used Doe and Bronco suede in red, light gray, black, brown (rust), and teal (blue)

- Two pieces of chamois, each 2 feet by 2 feet

- Ruler

- Sharp scissors

- Pastel pencil in white; we used Conté à Paris

- Fabric glue; we used Slomons Stitchless Fabric Glue

- 2-inch sponge brush

- Conchas, about 2 inches across at their widest point

- Glitter paint; we used Tulip Glitter Pen in multi

1.   Prepare duster by washing and drying; also wash and dry synthetic suede and chamois. Start by making five suede stars. The five stars will be progressively smaller in size and fit one inside the other. First decide the order for the colors of the stars. Then, starting with the color for the largest star and working on the wrong side of the suede fabric, cut a square 12 inches by 12 inches. Repeat this with each color, working from largest to smallest. The second square should be 10 inches by 10 inches; the third, 8 by 8; the fourth, 6 by 6; and the fifth, 4 by 4.

2.   For each square, draw freehand with pastel pencil a five-point star that just fits within its area.

3.   After all squares have a star drawn on them, cut out the outlined star on each square.

4. You are now ready to begin affixing the stars to each other. Start with the second largest star and work down to the smallest star. Place a small amount of glue on the wrong side of the second largest star. Use dampened sponge brush to brush the glue to the edge of the star.

5. Affix the second largest star inside the largest star. Be careful to glue the edge of the star securely. Precise placement of the star is not necessary. Repeat steps 4 and 5 with each progressively smaller star until all five stars are glued and secured, forming one large piece. Set aside.

6. Lay the duster flat to decide where you want to affix the chamois piece that will be the backdrop for the star. You may want to keep the entire piece on the back of the duster, or you may want to bring part of the chamois around the side of the duster to the front. You may have to trim a bit of the chamois piece for fit. Also, you may want to place (but not glue) the star on the chamois to help you decide. Once you've decided, use a pastel pencil to sketch in guide marks.

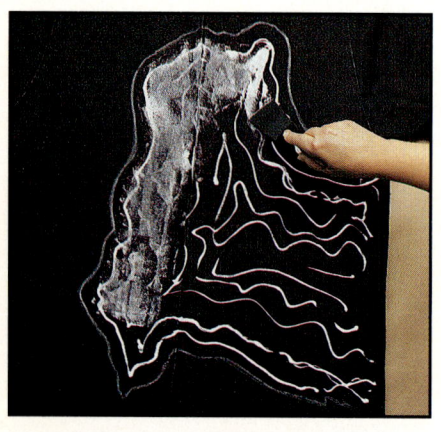

7. Remove the chamois. Place fabric glue on the duster where the chamois will go. Use dampened sponge brush to spread the glue on the denim.

8. Press the chamois into place. Be careful to affix every bit of the edge of the chamois to the duster, working around the edge of the chamois and smoothing it as you go to eliminate as many bubbles and wrinkles as possible.

9. Now glue the star to the chamois. Place glue on the back of the star and spread with sponge brush as in step 4. Place the star on the chamois, working to affix every bit of the edge of the star. Be careful to keep the star smooth.

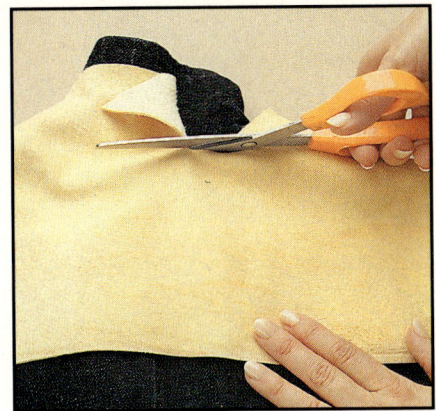

10.   Arrange the other piece of chamois at the top of the duster to make a yoke with a bottom line that runs straight across the back of the duster. (You may have to trim the bottom to get a straight line.) Trim the top of the chamois to conform to the shoulder seams and collar.

11.   As in steps 7 and 8, glue the chamois yoke to the duster, again spreading fabric glue on the duster with a sponge brush and being careful to keep the chamois as smooth as possible.

12.   Cut 12-inch-long lacings from the extra suede fabric. Using three colors per concha, knot the lacings through the conchas.

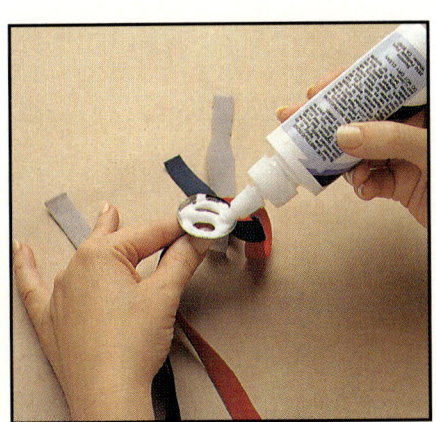

13.   Arrange (but do not glue) the conchas on the chamois until you like the overall look. When you're happy with the arrangement, apply glue to the back of one concha.

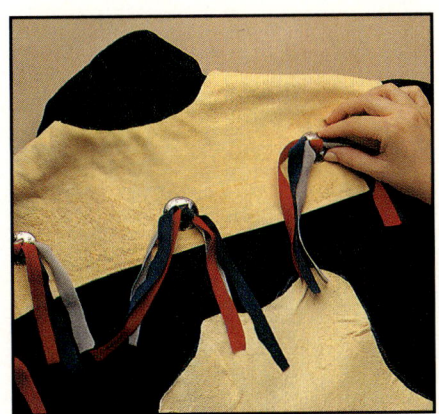

14.   Affix the concha to the chamois. Work with one concha at a time. Allow glue to dry. Heat-set glue either by ironing fabric on the wrong side with an iron set at medium heat for about 20 seconds or by placing fabric in dryer at medium setting for about 10 minutes.

15.   After glue has been heat-set, outline blue, black, and red stars with multi glitter paint. Start by outlining the blue star, then the black star, and ending with the red star. Allow the paint to dry.

Cityscape

For the city sophisticate (or the country cousin who just likes to visit), here's a jacket that evokes the glittering glamour of a big city. The skyline can be typical big city buildings, or it can be inspired by the skyline of San Francisco, New York City, or even London or Paris. The design of the jacket is easy to follow, and you'll feel confident changing it to accommodate your own favorite city. Read through the steps a couple of times and you'll be ready to go.

What You'll Need

- Denim jacket; we used dark blue

- Shirt board

- Silver pencil for sketching; we used Berol Verithin No. 753

- Ruler

- White iridescent glitter paint; we used Tulip Sparkles in crystal

- Palette (wax paper, paper plate, or top of a brush bin)

- Brushes; we used Tulip by Marx medium and small flat shaders

- Permanent fabric dyes; we used Grumbacher Galaxy in starwhite, silver, ginger, and gold

- White iridescent paint; we used Tulip Iridescent Fabric Paint in liquid pearl

- Slick dimensional paint; we used Tulip Slick Paint in black

- Glitter paints; we used Tulip Glitter Pens in gold, silver, and multi

- Permanent fabric marker in black; we used Niji Stylist II, size 03

- Rhinestones; we used 9 millimeter rhinestones by Puttin' on the Glitz

- Fabric glue; we used Slomons Stitchless Fabric Glue

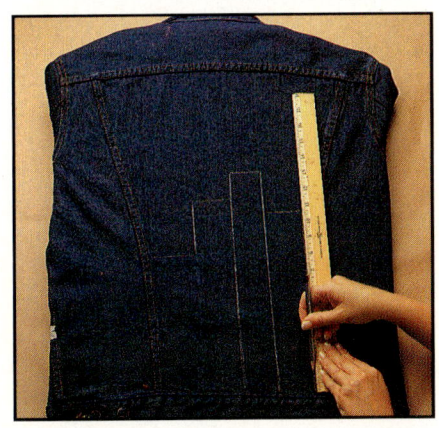

1. Prepare jacket by washing, drying, and taping to a shirt board with the back of the jacket on the wax side of the board. Consider your design and how many buildings you want. Sketch your design with a silver pencil; use a ruler to keep the lines straight. For a cityscape, you'll want a tall, vertical look, using smokestacks and antennae.

2. Sketch in the upper area with four clouds and a few birds. Sketch freehand for a casual look.

3. Place a dollop of white iridescent glitter paint on palette. Dampen medium shader brush; be sure to remove excess water from bristles, ferrule, and handle. Load brush with paint and paint three of the four clouds.

4. Place a dollop of starwhite permanent fabric dye on palette. Again dampen medium shader brush. Load brush with fabric dye and paint the fourth cloud.

5. When the fabric dye on the fourth cloud is almost dry, place a dollop of white iridescent paint on palette. Dampen medium shader brush and load with white iridescent paint. Brush iridescent paint into the fourth cloud, swirling to create a dimensional feeling.

6. Place black slick dimensional paint on palette. Dampen medium shader brush and load. Fill in the middle building. Place gold glitter paint on palette. Dampen and load small shader brush. Use one brush stroke for each large antenna on the middle building. Next, dampen and load medium shader with gold glitter paint and highlight the middle building.

7. Top off the middle building's antennae by applying a line of silver glitter paint directly from the tube. At the top of each silver antenna, place a small dot of multi glitter paint directly from the tube.

8. Place a dollop of ginger permanent fabric dye on palette. Dampen and load medium shader brush with ginger dye. Fill in the building on the right. After the building has been painted, dampen and load medium shader brush with silver glitter paint. Add a smokestack to the top of the ginger building.

9. For the smokestack's smoke, apply multi glitter paint directly from the tube. Smooth the paint out with your finger. The building on the left is done in the same way as the two previous buildings. It is painted with silver permanent fabric dye.

10. Using a ruler and a black permanent fabric marker, sketch in the windows and doors for the buildings. Outline the windows and doors in black slick paint, using a small flat shader brush.

11. Fill in the windows of the left-hand building with gold glitter paint, using a medium shader brush.

12. Go over the sketches of the birds in the sky with gold glitter paint, using a medium shader brush.

13. Paint shoulder seams, yoke seam, and bottom yoke with white iridescent glitter paint. Use the small shader brush for the seams and the medium shader brush for the bottom yoke.

14. When all paint is completely dry on the back, retape jacket on shirt board to paint the front. Use the same techniques you used to decorate the back.

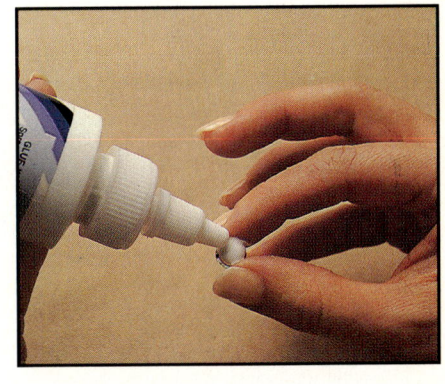

15. Embellish the jacket with rhinestones. Place a large dollop of fabric glue on each stone's flat side.

16. Place the rhinestone on the jacket and press in place to affix. Let paint dry 24 hours. Then heat-set garment by ironing on the wrong side at medium heat for about 20 seconds.

Tips and Variations

Try an old-fashioned skyline of Victorian houses or a streetscape of turn-of-the-century shops. A farm scene outlining a farmhouse, a silo, a barn, and fences in primary colors would work well for a child.

Victorian Lace

When denim goes romantic, this is how it looks. On the back, a panel of delicate flowers is framed by lace; on the front, we've placed individual flowers, lots of lace, and puffy little yo-yo trim. Although Victorian Lace involves more steps than the other projects in this book, the techniques used to create this appealing jacket are simple: no-sew appliqué, gluing, and basic painting. We also give you directions for making the fabric yo-yo. Making the yo-yos is a quick and easy process that you may want to finish before starting the jacket. Or, you can make them while waiting for the paint on the jacket to dry. Since there are so many steps, be sure to read all the directions several times before going to work.

What You'll Need

- Denim jacket; prewashed or stonewashed is best

- Fabric in a detailed flower pattern, washed and dried before using; the amount you'll need depends on how often the pattern repeats; we used one yard of 45-inch-wide fabric

- Adhesive web; we used Pellon Wonder-Under Transfer Web

- Ruler

- Sharp scissors

- Disappearing-ink pen

- Shirt board

- Dimensional paint; we used Tulip Fiber Fun! Fashion Paint in gold/yellow

- Palette (wax paper, paper plate, or top of a brush bin)

- Brush; we used Liquitex No. 10 Nylon Flat shader

- Lace in white and one other shade to complement your fabric, washed and dried before using; we used two yards of 1¼-inch-wide gathered lace in blue, one yard of 3¼-inch-wide double-edged flat lace in white, and two yards of 1¼-inch-wide gathered cotton lace in white

- Fabric glue; we used Slomons Stitchless Fabric Glue

- Glitter paint; we used Tulip Glitter Pen in gold

- Iridescent fabric paint in a shade to complement your fabric; we used Tulip Iridescent Fabric Pen in peach frost

- Five lace appliqués in colors to complement your fabric, snipped from scraps of lace if possible; we used four white appliqués and one mauve appliqué. Two of the white lace appliqués and the one mauve appliqué were about 3 inches in circumference; the other two white lace appliqués were about 1½ inches in circumference.

- Flat plastic circles of various sizes, such as the lid of a coffee can

- Needle and thread in a color to accompany your fabric

- Gems of various shapes and sizes

1. Wash and dry the jacket. Lay the jacket flat, back side up, and decide which area of the jacket's back you wish to cover with flower pattern fabric. Following the manufacturer's directions, affix adhesive web to the back of the fabric.

2. Measure the width of the area of the jacket you plan to cover with fabric. Closely trim a piece of fabric to fit the width.

3. Place the fabric over the area of the jacket you plan to cover. Using a disappearing-ink pen, mark where the fabric should be cut to fit the length of jacket area. Trim excess fabric.

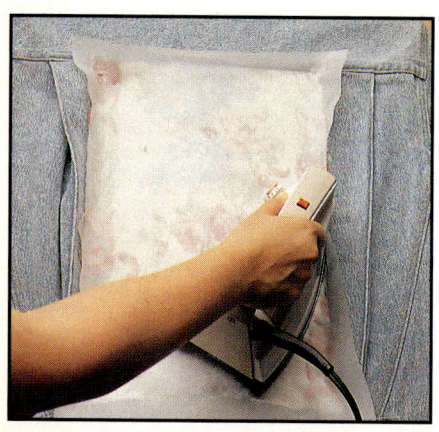

4. Remove the paper from the adhesive web. Iron the fabric onto the jacket. Be sure to seal all edges.

5. Tape the jacket to a shirt board. Place a dollop of Fiber Fun! gold/yellow dimensional paint on palette. Dampen brush slightly, wiping excess water from bristles, ferrule, and handle. Starting from the top of the jacket, paint top yoke area from shoulder to shoulder and collar seam to yoke seam. Continue painting, covering the area between the slanted seams and the fabric. Finally, paint the bottom yoke. Allow the paint to dry.

6. Measure the length of the top yoke's seam and cut a piece of 3¼-inch-wide white flat lace to fit the length of this seam. Set aside. Place fabric glue along the bottom of the top yoke. Spread the glue with your fingers to cover an area as wide as the white flat lace.

7. Affix lace to yoke seam.

8. Applying gold glitter paint directly from the tube, outline all the outer edges of the fabric to reseal the edges.

9. Again applying paint directly from the tube, highlight details within the fabric panel using both gold glitter paint and peach iridescent paint. Allow the paint to dry.

10. You are now ready to "frame" the fabric panel with two vertical columns of narrow white lace. First, flatten the gathered lace; use scissors to snip along the ruffle casing. Remove casing. Flatten enough lace to cover the slanted seams on either side of the fabric as well as the side seams of the bottom yoke. Smooth out lace, iron if necessary.

11. Place a line of fabric glue along the slanted seams and the side seams of the bottom yoke. Place flattened lace on slanted seams and side seams of bottom yoke, pressing gently to affix.

12. Cut enough gathered white lace to cover the two horizontal seams of the bottom yoke. Place a line of fabric glue on the seams. Place the gathered lace on the seams and press gently to affix to the jacket. Allow the glue to dry.

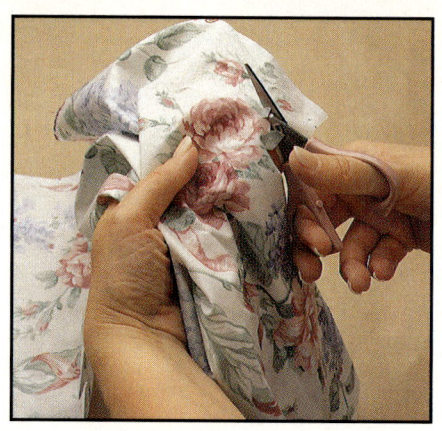

13. When the back decorations are completely dry, remove the jacket from the shirt board and retape to work on the front of the jacket. On a piece of paper, trace an outline of the right shoulder area that will be covered with a piece of pattern fabric. Cut a piece of fabric treated with adhesive web to fit the outline. Remove adhesive web paper and iron fabric to shoulder.

14. Using scissors, cut two small flower appliqués from the pattern fabric treated with adhesive web. Remove adhesive paper and iron these two appliqués on the jacket, being careful to seal all edges. We placed one flower on the left pocket and one flower "growing" out of the left pocket.

15. Snip all five lace appliqués from scrap lace. Set aside three white lace appliqués (two small and one large).

16. Working with one appliqué at a time, apply fabric glue to the back of one large white lace appliqué and the mauve lace appliqué. Place the mauve appliqué at the left shoulder and the white appliqué on the right pocket.

17. Using gold glitter paint directly from the tube, outline the lace appliqué flowers, the leaves of the fabric on the right shoulder, and the leaves of the fabric appliqués at the left pocket. Using peach iridescent paint, highlight the details of the flowers on the fabric. Allow the paint to dry.

18. On the seam of the left pocket, place a line of fabric glue. Affix gathered blue lace to outline the pocket, pressing gently.

19. Flatten enough blue lace (as in step 10) to "frame" the fabric on the right shoulder and to outline adjacent sleeve armhole. Place a line of fabric glue around the pattern fabric on the right shoulder and on the seam of the sleeve armhole. Place flattened blue lace on glue, pressing gently to affix to the jacket. If necessary, stabilize the lace on the armhole with straight pins until the glue dries.

20. While the glue is drying, make yo-yos. Place remaining pattern fabric wrong side up on a flat surface. Using a disappearing-ink pen, trace three circles of different sizes. A coffee can lid or a smaller top can serve as a guide while you trace.

21. Using scissors, cut out each circle. Turn over a ⅛-inch hem. Secure this hem with a running stitch.

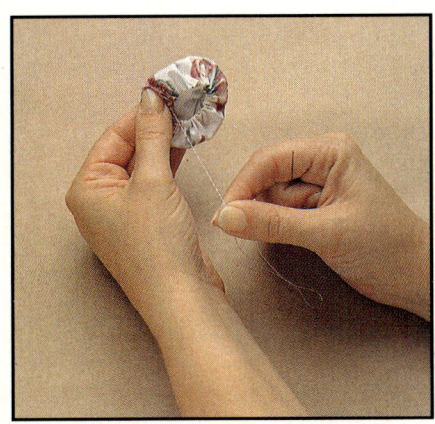

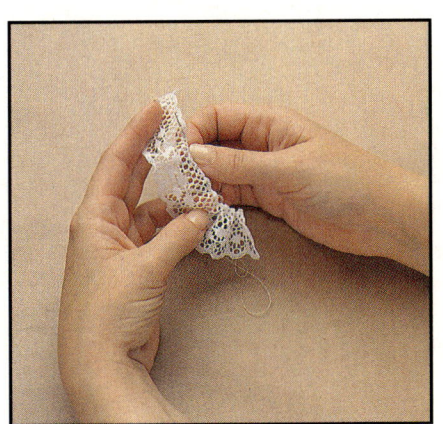

22. After sewing the hem, pull the thread close to evenly gather the fabric, creating the yo-yo's puffy, rounded effect. Knot the thread.

23. To make a lace yo-yo, cut a length of flattened narrow white lace. Stitch and draw it into a circle as in steps 21 and 22.

24. Apply fabric glue to the backs of the yo-yos. Place three yo-yos on the jacket below the right pocket, pressing gently to affix the yo-yos to the jacket. Place one yo-yo at the left shoulder.

25. Apply fabric glue to the back of a small white lace appliqué. Place the appliqué on the left pocket in the lower right corner. Outline the appliqué with gold glitter paint.

26. Finish the front of the jacket by gluing various gems, such as half pearls, rhinestones, and colored navettes, to the jacket. Place them along the shoulders and wherever else you wish to "fill in" the jacket. To glue the gems, place a dab of glue on the back of each gem and press it into place on the jacket.

27. After the glue has dried on the front of the jacket, turn the jacket over. Working with one appliqué at a time, apply fabric glue to the final two white lace appliqués. Place the appliqués on the top yoke where the yoke meets the sleeve, one on each side. When all glue and paint have dried, heat-set glue by ironing on the wrong side of jacket at medium heat for about 20 seconds.

Tips and Variations

Get a Southwestern feel—and a totally different look—by using a geometric print in desert shades. Substitute braid or fringe trim for lace and conchas for navettes.

Try a child's jacket made with circus or animal fabric and trimmed with braid or ball fringe. Check the drapery section in a department store for wonderful, elaborate trims.